General Instructions

ABBREVIATIONS

alt	= alternate	**P**	= purl
beg	= beginning	**pat**	= pattern
cont	= continue(ity)	**psso**	= pass slipped st over
dec	= decrease	**rem**	= remaining
mm	= millimeter(s)	**rep**	= repeat
g	= gram(s)	**rnd(s)**	= round(s)
in(s)	= inch(es)	**sl**	= slip
st(s)	= stitch(es)	**Sl1(K)**	= slip next st knitwise
inc	= increase 1 stitch by	**Sl1P**	= slip next st purlwise
knitting into front and back of		**tog**	= together
next stitch		**yo**	= yarn over
K	= knit	**0**	= no sts, times or rows

* = The star symbol is a repeat sign and means that you follow the printed instructions from the first * until you reach the second *. You will then repeat from * to * the given number of times which **does not** include the first time. The ** and *** are used in the same way.

{ } = Brackets mean that the enclosed instructions are to be worked the number of times stated after the brackets.

Work even = Work without increasing or decreasing in the established pattern.

Right Side = Refers to the front of the piece.

Wrong Side = Refers to the back of the piece.

YARN

The items shown can be made with any yarn in the weight specified as long as the correct gauge can be obtained.

It is best to refer to the yardage to determine how many skeins to purchase.

GAUGE

Remember, in order for your item to be the correct size, it is not the brand of yarn that matters, but the GAUGE that is important.

Exact gauge is **essential** for proper fit. Before beginning your item, make a sample swatch using the yarn and needle specified. After completing the swatch, measure it, counting your stitches and rows carefully. If your swatch is larger or smaller than specified, **make another, changing needle size to get the correct gauge.** Keep trying until you find the size needles that will give you the specified gauge. Once proper gauge is obtained, measure width of item approximately every 3" to be sure gauge remains consistent.

Note: Never put an iron directly on yarns containing synthetic fibers. If pressing is required before assembly, lay each piece Right Side down on a clean, flat surface and pin to size using rust proof pins. Cover with a damp cloth and leave to dry.

KNITTING NEEDLE CONVERSION CHART

U.S. Sizes	17	15	13	11	-	-	10½	10	9	8	7	6	5	4	3	-	2	1	0	-
Metric (mm)	12.75	10	9	8	7.5	7	6.5	6	5.5	5	4.5	4	3.75	3.5	3.25	3	2.75	2.25	2	1.75
Cdn. / U.K. Sizes	-	000	00	0	1	2	3	4	5	6	7	8	9	-	10	11	12	13	14	15

PATTERN RATINGS

■□□□ **BEGINNER** — Projects for first-time knitters using basic stitches. Minimal shaping.

■■□□ **EASY** — Projects using basic stitches, repetitive stitch patterns, simple color changes, and simple shaping and finishing.

■■■□ **INTERMEDIATE** — Projects with a variety of stitches and techniques such as basic cables and lace, simple intarsia and double pointed needles.

■■■■ **EXPERIENCED** — Projects using advanced techniques and stitches such as short rows, fair isle, more intricate intarsia and cables and numerous color changes.

Yarn Weight Symbol	Types of Yarns in Category
1 SUPER FINE	Sock, Baby, Fingering
2 FINE	Sport, Baby
3 LIGHT	DK, Light Worsted
4 MEDIUM	Worsted, Afghan, Aran
5 BULKY	Chunky, Craft, Rug
6 SUPER BULKY	Bulky, Roving

SIZE

One size: To fit average lady.

MATERIALS

Sample made with
Patons® Classic Merino Wool (100 g / 3.5 oz)

Main Color: #77010 Natural Marl
Contrast A: #00202 Aran

Hat and Scarf		
Main Color (MC) (Ragg)	**2**	**balls**
Contrast A (Cream)	**1**	**ball**

Sizes 4.5 mm (U.S. 7) knitting needles for Hat and
6.5 mm (U.S. 10½) circular knitting needle 32" [90 cm]
long for scarf **or size needed to obtain gauge.**

GAUGE SWATCH

20 sts and 26 rows = 4" [10 cm] with 4.5 mm needles in
stocking st.

ABBREVIATIONS

alt = alternate
beg = beginning
cont = continue(ity)
dec = decrease
inc = increase 1 stitch by
knitting into front and back
of next stitch
K = knit
K2tog = Knit 2 stitches
together

psso = pass slipped st over
rem = remaining
rep = repeat
Sl1P = slip next st purlwise
st(s) = stitch(es)
yb = bring yarn to back of
work
yf = bring yarn to front of
work
yfwd = yarn forward

INSTRUCTIONS

Hat

With Ragg and 4.5 mm needles cast on 101 sts.
1st row: (Right side). Knit.
2nd row: Knit.
3rd and 4th rows: With Cream, knit.
5th and 6th rows: With Ragg, knit.

7th and 8th rows: With Cream, K1. *yf. Sl1P.
yb. K1. Rep from * to end of row.
9th and 10th rows: With Ragg, knit.
11th row: With Cream, K1. *yfwd. K2tog. Rep
from * to end of row.
12th row: With Cream, knit.

13th to 16th rows: With Ragg, knit.
17th to 20th rows: As 7th to 10th rows, inc 1 st in centre of last row. 102 sts. Break Cream.
With Ragg, beg with a knit row work 8 rows in stocking st.

Crown shaping: Next row: K2. K2tog. *K15. Sl1. K1. psso. K1. K2tog. Rep from * 3 times more. K15. Sl1. K1. psso. K1. 92 sts.
Work 3 rows even in stocking st.
Next row: K2. K2tog. *K13. Sl1. K1. psso. K1. K2tog. Rep from * 3 times more. K13. Sl1. K1. psso. K1. 82 sts.
Work 3 rows even in stocking st.
Next row: K2. K2tog. *K11. Sl1. K1. psso. K1. K2tog. Rep from * 3 times more. K11. Sl1. K1. psso. K1. 72 sts.
Next row: Purl.
Cont in this manner, dec 10 sts every alt row, until 22 sts rem.
Next row: K2. K2tog. (Sl1. K2tog. psso. K1) 3 times. Sl1. K2tog. psso. K2tog. K1. 12 sts.
Next row: Purl.
Next row: (K2tog) 6 times. 6 sts.
Break yarn and thread through rem sts. Fasten off. Sew centre back seam.

Scarf

With Ragg and circular needle cast on 173 sts. **Do not join.** Working back and forth across needle, proceed as follows:
1st row: (Right side). Knit.
2nd to 4th rows: Knit.
5th and 6th rows: With Cream, K1. *yf. Sl1P. yb. K1. Rep from * to end of row.
7th to 10th rows: With Ragg, knit.
11th row: With Cream, K1. *yfwd. K2tog. Rep from * to end of row.
12th row: With Cream, knit.
13th and 14th rows: With Ragg, knit.
15th and 16th rows: With Cream, knit.
17th and 18th rows: With Ragg, K1. *yf. Sl1P. yb. K1. Rep from * to end of row.

19th and 20th rows: With Cream, knit.
21st row: With Ragg, K1. *yfwd. K2tog. Rep from * to end of row.
22nd row: With Ragg, knit.
23rd and 24th rows: With Cream, knit.
25th and 26th rows: With Ragg, knit.
27th and 28th rows: With Cream, K1. *yf. Sl1P. yb. K1. Rep from * to end of row.
29th to 32nd rows: With Ragg, knit.
33rd and 34th rows: With Cream, K1. *yf. Sl1P. yb. K1. Rep from * to end of row.
35th and 36th rows: With Ragg, knit.
37th and 38th rows: With Cream, knit.
39th row: With Ragg, K1. *yfwd. K2tog. Rep from * to end of row.
40th row: With Ragg, knit.
41st and 42nd rows: With Cream, knit.
43rd and 44th rows: With Ragg, K1. *yf. Sl1P. yb. K1. Rep from * to end of row.
45th and 46th rows: With Cream, knit.
47th and 48th rows: With Ragg, knit.
49th row: With Cream, K1. *yfwd. K2tog. Rep from * to end of row.
50th row: With Cream, knit.
51st to 54th rows: With Ragg, knit.
55th and 56th rows: With Cream, K1. *yf. Sl1P. yb. K1. Rep from * to end of row.
57th to 60th rows: With Ragg, knit.
With Ragg, bind off knitwise.

Striped Socks, Cap and Scarf

SIZES

Socks
Finished Foot Length

Small	9"	[23	cm]
Medium	9½"	[24	cm]
Large	10½"	[26.5	cm]

Cap: One Size to fit average adult.

Scarf: Approx 9" [23 cm] wide x 64" [162.5 cm] long.

MATERIALS

Sample made with Patons® Kroy Socks (50 g / 1.75 oz)

Main Color: #54044 Mercury
Contrast A: #54040 Coal
Contrast B: #54008 Muslin

SOCKS

Sizes	S	M	L	
Main Color (MC) (Gray)	2	2	2	balls
Contrast A (Black)	1	1	1	ball
Contrast B (Cream)	1	1	1	ball

CAP

Main Color (MC) (Gray)	2	balls
Contrast A (Black)	1	ball
Contrast B (Cream)	1	ball

SCARF

Main Color (MC) (Gray)	7	balls
Contrast A (Black)	1	ball
Contrast B (Cream)	1	ball

Set of four double pointed knitting needles size 2.75 mm (U.S. 2) for Socks and Cap. Set of four double pointed knitting needles size 3.25 mm (U.S. 3) for Cap. Pair of size 3.25 mm (U.S. 3) knitting needles for Scarf **or size needed to obtain gauge.**

GAUGE SWATCH

Socks: 34 sts and 44 rows = 4" [10 cm] with 2.75 mm needles in stocking st.

Cap or Scarf: 28 sts and 36 rows = 4" [10 cm] with 3.25 mm needles in stocking st.

Striped Socks, Cap and Scarf

ABBREVIATIONS

alt = alternate
approx = approximately
beg = beginning
cont = continue(ity)
dec = decrease
K = knit
K2tog = knit 2 stitches together
P = purl
P2tog = purl 2 stitches together
psso = pass slipped st over
rem = remaining
rep = repeat
rnd = round
Sl1 = Slip next stitch knitwise
st(s) = stitch(es)
tog = together

INSTRUCTIONS

Socks

The instructions are written for smallest size. If changes are necessary for larger sizes the instructions will be written thus { }. When only one number is given, it applies to both sizes. For ease in working, circle all numbers pertaining to your size.

With Black, cast on 68 sts **loosely.** Divide sts into 18 sts on first needle, 32 sts on second needle and 18 sts on third needle. Join in rnd, placing a marker on first st.

**Work 4 rnds in (K2. P2) ribbing.
With Gray, work 4 rnds in (K2. P2) ribbing.
With Cream, work 4 rnds in (K2. P2) ribbing.
With Gray, work 4 rnds in (K2. P2) ribbing.
Rep last 16 rnds once more.
With Black, work 4 rnds in (K2. P2) ribbing.**
With Gray, knit in rnds until work from beg measures 7½" [19 cm].

Make heel: Divide 32 sts on second needle onto 2 needles and leave for instep. Knit 18 sts off first needle onto end of third needle. 36 sts for heel.
Next row: (Wrong side). K1. P16. P2tog. P16. K1. 35 sts. Break Gray.
Next row: With Black, *K1. Sl1. Rep from * to last st. K1.
Next row: Purl.
With Black, rep last 2 rows until heel measures 2½" [6 cm], ending with Wrong side facing for next row.

Shape heel: 1st row: K1. P17. P2tog. P1. Turn.
2nd row: K3. Sl1. K1. psso. K1. Turn.
3rd row: P4. P2tog. P1. Turn.
4th row: K5. Sl1. K1. psso. K1. Turn.
5th row: P6. P2tog. P1. Turn.
6th row: K7. Sl1. K1. psso. K1. Turn.
7th row: P8. P2tog. P1. Turn.
8th row: K9. Sl1. K1. psso. K1. Turn.
9th row: P10. P2tog. P1. Turn.
10th row: K11. Sl1. K1. psso. K1. Turn.
11th row: P12. P2tog. P1. Turn.
12th row: K13. Sl1. K1. psso. K1. Turn.
13th row: P14. P2tog. P1. Turn.
14th row: K15. Sl1. K1. psso. K1. Turn.
15th row: P16. P2tog. P1. Turn.
16th row: K17. Sl1. K1. psso. K1. 19 sts. Break Black.

Shape Instep: With Right side of work facing, Gray and first needle, pick up and knit 18 sts along left side of heel. With second needle, knit across 32 sts for instep. With third needle, pick up and knit 18 sts along right side of heel. Knit first 10 sts from heel onto end of third needle. Slip rem 9 sts from heel onto beg of first needle. 87 sts are now divided as 27 sts on first needle, 32 sts on second needle and 28 sts on third needle.
1st rnd: *1st needle:* Knit to last 4 sts. K2tog. K2. ***2nd needle:*** Knit. ***3rd needle:*** K2. Sl1. K1. psso. Knit to end of needle.
2nd rnd: Knit.

Striped Socks, Cap and Scarf

Rep last 2 rnds until there are 63 sts divided as 15 sts on first needle, 32 sts on second needle and 16 sts on third needle.

Cont even until foot from picked up sts at heel measures 5½ {**6-7**}" [14 {**15-18**} cm].
Next rnd: Knit, dec 1 st at center. 62 sts.

Shape toe: With Black, **1st rnd:** *1st needle:* Knit to last 3 sts. K2tog. K1. *2nd needle:* K1. Sl1. K1. psso. Knit to last 3 sts. K2tog. K1. *3rd needle:* K1. Sl1. K1. psso. Knit to end of needle.
2nd rnd: Knit.
With Black, rep last 2 rnds until there are 18 sts divided as 5 sts on first needle, 9 sts on second needle and 4 sts on third needle. Slip sts on first needle onto third needle.

With Black, graft 2 sets of 9 sts tog for toe (see Grafting Diagram). Block on sock blockers or press lightly on Wrong side with a damp cloth.

Cap

With Black and set of four smaller needles, cast on 132 sts loosely.
Divide sts into 44 sts on each of 3 needles. Join in rnd, placing a marker on first st.

Work from ** to ** as given for Socks.

Change to set of four larger needles and knit in rnds until work from beg measures 7" [18 cm].

Shape crown: 1st rnd: K14. *K2tog. K2. Sl1. K1. psso. K27. Rep from * twice more. K2tog. K2. Sl1. K1. psso. K13.
2nd and alt rnds: Knit.
3rd rnd: K13. *K2tog. K2. Sl1. K1. psso. K25. Rep from * twice more. K2tog. K2. Sl1. K1. psso. K12.
5th rnd: K12. *K2tog. K2. Sl1. K1. psso. K23. Rep from * twice more. K2tog. K2. Sl1. K1. psso. K11.

Cont in this manner, dec 8 sts evenly around every following alt rnd until there are 20 sts. Break yarn leaving a long end. Draw end through rem sts tightly and fasten securely.

Scarf

With Black, cast on 72 sts.
1st row: (Right side). K2. *P2. K4. Rep from * to last 4 sts. P2. K2.
2nd row: P2. *K2. P4. Rep from * to last 4 sts. K2. P2.
These 2 rows form rib pat.
Rep last 2 rows once more.
With Gray, work 4 rows rib pat.
With Cream, work 4 rows rib pat.
With Gray, work 4 rows rib pat.
Rep last 16 rows once more.
With Black, work 4 rows rib pat.
With Gray, cont in rib pat until work from beg measures 61" [155 cm], ending on a 2nd row.
With Black, work 4 rows rib pat.
With Gray, work 4 rows rib pat.
With Cream, work 4 rows rib pat.
With Gray, work 4 rows rib pat.
Rep last 16 rows once more.
With Black, work 4 rows rib pat. Bind off in ribbing.

Grafting Diagram

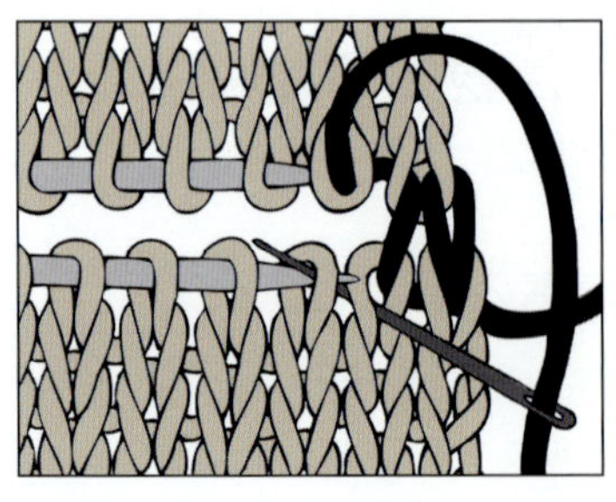
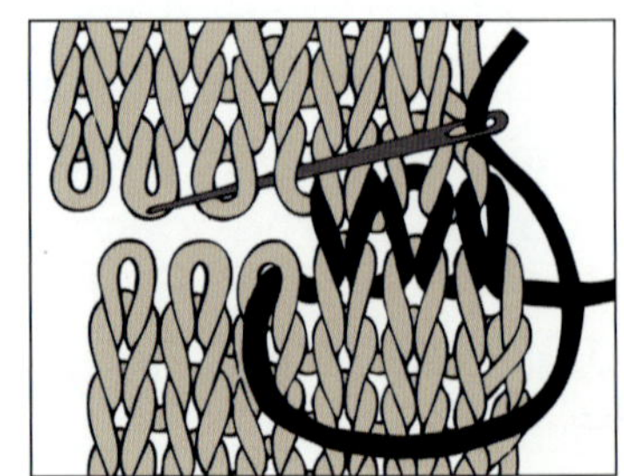

EASY

SIZE

One Size to fit child 3 to 5 years.

MATERIALS

Sample made with Patons® Decor (100 g / 3.5 oz)

Red Version
Contrast A: #01714 Barn Red
Contrast B: #01713 Orange

Blue Version
Contrast A: #01642 Rich Periwinkle
Contrast B: #01641 Periwinkle

RED VERSION		
Contrast A (Red)	1	**ball**
Contrast B (Orange)	1	**ball**
BLUE VERSION		
Contrast A (Dark Blue)	1	**ball**
Contrast B (Blue)	1	**ball**

Size 6.5 mm (U.S. 10½) knitting needles **or size needed to obtain gauge.**

GAUGE SWATCH

13 sts and 18 rows = 4" [10 cm] in stocking stitch with 2 strands of yarn.

ABBREVIATIONS

alt = alternate
approx = approximately
beg = beginning
cont = continue(ity)
dec = decrease
inc = increase 1 stitch by knitting into front and back of next stitch
K = knit
K2tog = knit 2 stitches together

rem = remaining
rep = repeat
st(s) = stitch(es)
tog = together

INSTRUCTIONS

Right Earflap: **With 1 strand each of A and B, cast on 5 sts.

1st row: (Wrong side). Knit.

2nd row: Inc 1 st in first st. Knit to last 2 sts. Inc 1 st in next st. K1.

Rep last 2 rows until there are 13 sts.

Work 3 rows even.

Next row: Inc 1 st in first st. Knit to last 2 sts. Inc 1 st in next st. K1.

Rep last 4 rows twice more. 19 sts.

Work 1 row even.**

Next row: Inc 1 st in first st. Knit to end of row.

Work 1 row even.

Rep last 2 rows once more. 21 sts.

Next row: Inc 1 st in first st. Knit to last 2 sts. Inc 1 st in next st. K1. 23 sts.

Work 1 row even.

Break yarn. Leave these sts on a spare needle.

Left Earflap: Work from ** to ** as given for Right Earflap.

Next row: Knit to last 2 sts. Inc 1 st in next st. K1.

Work 1 row even.

Rep last 2 rows once more. 21 sts.

Next row: Inc 1 st in first st. Knit to last 2 sts. Inc 1 st in next st. K1. 23 sts.

Work 1 row even.

Joining row: (Right side). Cast on 2 sts. Knit these 2 sts and 23 sts of Right Earflap. **Turn.** Cast on 11 sts. **Turn.** K23 of Left Earflap. **Turn.** Cast on 2 sts. 61 sts.

Next row: Knit.

Beg with a knit row, proceed in stocking st until work from joining row measures 4" [10 cm], ending with Right side facing for next row.

Shape top (worked in garter st): 1st row: K1. *K2tog. K8. Rep from * to end of row. 55 sts.

2nd and alt rows: Knit.

3rd row: K1. *K2tog. K7. Rep from * to end of row. 49 sts.

5th row: K1. *K2tog. K6. Rep from * to end of row. 43 sts.

Cont in this manner, dec 6 sts evenly across every following alt row until there are 13 sts.

Next row: (Wrong side). (K2tog) 6 times. K1. Break yarn leaving a long end. Draw end through rem sts and fasten securely. Sew center back seam.

Pom-pom (Optional)

Wind 1 strand each of MC and A around 4 fingers approx 60 times. Remove from fingers and tie tightly in center. Cut through each side of loops. Trim to a smooth round shape. Sew to top of Hat.

Pom-pom Diagram

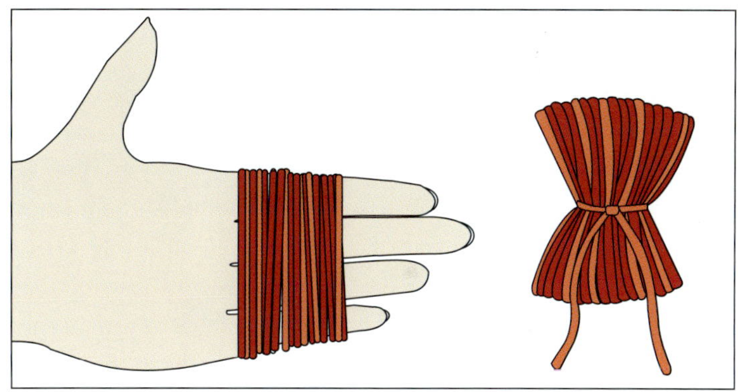

Ties: Cut twenty-four 20" {51 cm} lengths of MC and A. Taking 12 strands of each color tog, draw halfway through center of lower edge of Earflap. Divide strands into 3 groups of 8 and braid into tie. Secure ends and trim evenly.

Braid

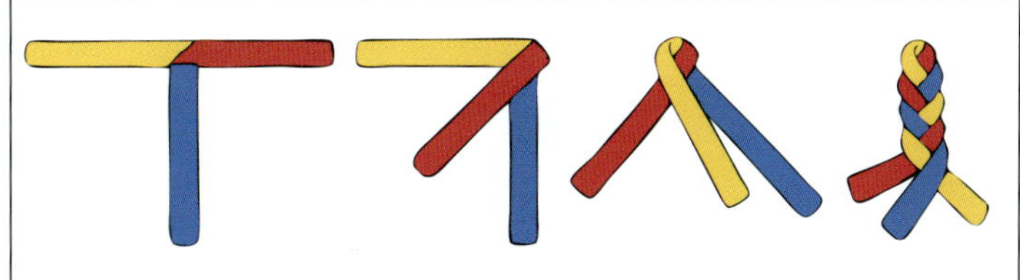

 **EASY**

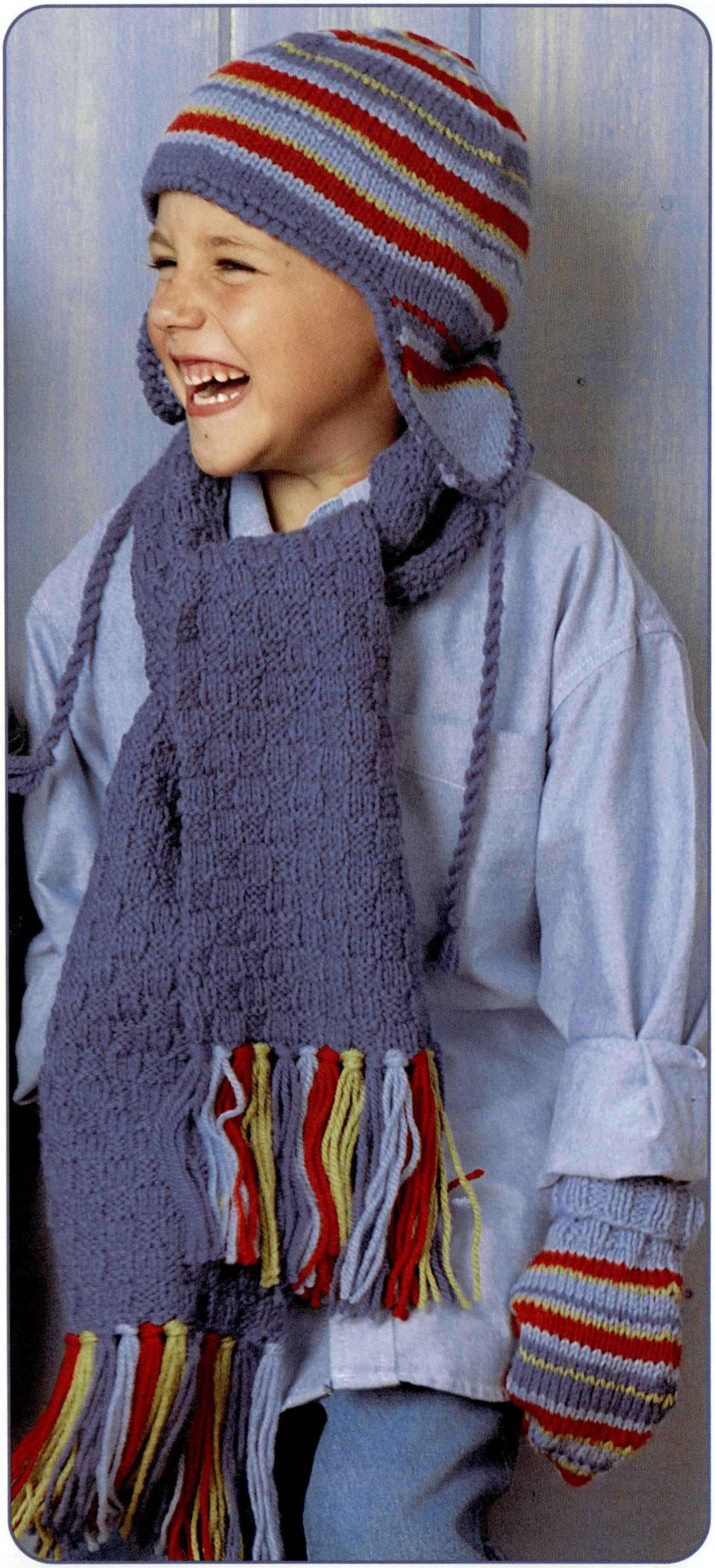

SIZES

Hat and Mittens
To fit child 4-6 years or 8-10 years.

Scarf: Measures approx 7" x 44 " [18 x 112 cm].

MATERIALS

**Sample made with
Patons® Decor** (100 g / 3.5 oz) 
Hat and Mittens
Main Color: (#01641 Periwinkle)
Contrast A: (#01642 Rich Periwinkle)
Contrast B: (#01714 Barn Red)
Contrast C: (#01607 Pale Olive)

Scarf
Main Color: (#01642 Rich Periwinkle)

Size	4-6	8-10	yrs
HAT			
Main Color (MC) (Blue)	1	1	ball
Contrast A (Dark Blue)	1	1	ball
Contrast B (Red)	1	1	ball
Contrast C (Green)	1	1	ball
MITTENS			
Main Color (MC) (Blue)	1	1	ball
Contrast A (Dark Blue)	1	1	ball
Contrast B (Red)	1	1	ball
Contrast C (Green)	1	1	ball
SCARF			

Main Color (MC)
(#01642 Rich Periwinkle)   **2   balls**
Small quantities of Contrast A, B and C for fringe.

Sizes 4 mm (U.S. 6) and 4.5 mm (U.S. 7) knitting needles **or size needed to obtain gauge.**
Size 4 mm (U.S. G or 6) crochet hook for Hat and fringe for Scarf.

Funky Stripes and Checks Set

GAUGE SWATCH

Hat and Scarf: 20 sts and 26 rows = 4" [10 cm] with larger needles in stocking st.

Mittens: 21 sts and 28 rows = 4" [10 cm] with smaller needles in stocking st.

ABBREVIATIONS

alt = alternate
approx = approximately
beg = beginning
cont = continue(ity)
dec = decrease
inc = increase 1 stitch by knitting into front and back of next stitch
K = knit
K2tog = knit 2 stitches together

P = purl
pat = pattern
P2tog = purl 2 stitches together
psso = pass slipped stitch over
rep = repeat
Sl1 = slip next stitch knitwise
st(s) = stitch(es)
rem = remaining
tog = together

INSTRUCTIONS

The instructions are written for the smaller size. If changes are necessary for larger size the instructions will be written thus { }. When only one number is given, it applies to both sizes. For ease in working, circle all numbers pertaining to your size.

Hat

Ear Flap (make 2): With Blue and larger needles, cast on 11 sts.

1st row: (Right side). Knit.
2nd row: Inc 1 st in first st purlwise. Purl to last 2 sts. Inc 1 st in next st purlwise. P1.
3rd row: Inc 1 st in first st. Knit to last 2 sts. Inc 1 st in next st. K1.
4th row: Purl.
Rep last 2 rows 4 times more. 23 sts.
Next row: (Right side). With Green, knit.
With Red, beg with a purl row, work 3 rows stocking st.
With Blue, beg with a knit row, work 2 rows stocking st.

With Dark Blue, beg with a knit row, work 2 rows stocking st.
With Red, knit 1 row.
With Dark Blue, purl 1 row.
Break yarn of First Ear Flap. **Do not** break yarn of Second Ear Flap. Leave sts on a spare needle.

Body of Hat: Joining row: With Dark Blue and larger needles, cast on 6 sts. Knit these sts and 23 sts of Second Ear Flap. **Turn.** Cast on 32 {**36**} sts. **Turn.** K23 of First Ear Flap. **Turn.** Cast on 6 sts. 90 {**94**} sts.
Beg with a purl row, work 3 rows stocking st.

Proceed in stocking st Stripe Pat as follows:
With Blue, work 2 rows.
With Red, work 3 rows.
With Green, work 1 row.
With Blue, work 3 rows.
With Dark Blue, work 1 row.
With Blue, work 1 row.
With Green, work 1 row.
With Red, work 3 rows.
With Blue, work 2 rows.
With Dark Blue, work 2 rows.
With Green, work 1 row.
With Dark Blue, work 4 rows.
These 24 rows form Stripe Pat.

Cont even in Stripe Pat until work from joining row measures 4 1/2 {**4 3/4**}" [11.5 {**12**} cm], ending with a purl row and dec 4 {**8**} sts evenly across last row. 86 sts.

Shape top: Next row: K2. Sl1. K1. psso. *K15. K2tog. K2. Sl1. K1. psso. Rep from * twice more. K15. K2tog. K2. 78 sts.
Next row: Purl.
Next row: K2. Sl1. K1. psso. *K13. K2tog. K2. Sl1. K1. psso. Rep from * twice more. K13. K2tog. K2. 70 sts.
Next row: Purl.
Next row: K2. Sl1. K1. psso. *K11. K2tog. K2. Sl1. K1. psso. Rep from * twice more. K11. K2tog. K2. 62 sts.
Next row: Purl.

Funky Stripes and Checks Set

Cont in this manner, dec 8 sts evenly across next and every alt row until there are 30 sts.

Next row: K2. Sl1. K1. psso. *K1. K2tog. K2. Sl1. K1. psso. Rep from * twice more. K1. K2tog. K2. 22 sts.

Next row: P2. *P2tog. P2. Rep from * to end of row. 17 sts.

Break yarn leaving a long end. Draw end through rem sts and fasten securely. Sew center back seam.

Edging: With Right side of work facing, Dark Blue and crochet hook, work 1 row of Single Crochet evenly around outer edge of Hat working into every 4 out of 5 sts to keep edge even. Join with slip stitch to first single crochet. (See Diagrams on page 17).

Next row: Working from **left** to right, instead of from **right** to left as usual, work 1 Reverse Single Crochet in each single crochet across (see Diagram on page 17). Join with slip stitch to first single crochet. Fasten off.

Ties: Make twisted cords by cutting 3 lengths of yarn 24" [61 cm] long. Taking all strands tog, hold one end and with someone holding other end, twist strands to the right until they begin to curl. Fold the 2 ends tog and tie in a knot so they will not unravel. The strands will now twist themselves tog. (See Twisted Cords Diagram on page 17).

Mittens

Right Mitten: **With Blue and smaller needles, cast on 36 {**40**} sts.

1st row: (Right side). *K2. P2. Rep from * to end of row.

2nd row: *K2. P2. Rep from * to end of row. These 2 rows form (K2. P2) ribbing.

Work a further 16 rows in (K2. P2) ribbing.

Proceed in Stocking St Stripe Pat as given for Hat for 6 {**8**} rows.**

Keeping cont of Stripe Pat, shape thumb gusset as follows:

1st row: K19 {**21**}. Inc 1 st in each of next 2 sts. Knit to end of row.

2nd row: Purl.

3rd row: K19 {**21**}. Inc 1 st in next st. K2. Inc 1 st in next st. Knit to end of row.

4th row: Purl.

5th row: K19 {**21**}. Inc 1 st in next st. K4. Inc 1 st in next st. Knit to end of row.

6th row: Purl.

Cont in this manner, having 2 sts more between incs for thumb gusset every alt row until there are 46 {**50**} sts.

Next row: Purl.

Make thumb: Next row: K31 {**33**}. **Turn.** Cast on 1 st. P12 (including cast on st). **Turn.** Cast on 1 st. Cont in Stripe Pat on these 13 sts for 2 {**2**1/4**}" [5 {**5.5**} cm], ending with a purl row.

Next row: K1. *K2tog. Rep from * to end of row. 7 sts. Break yarn leaving a long end. Draw end through rem sts and fasten securely. Sew thumb seam.

Remainder of Mitten: With Right side of work facing, join appropriate yarn to last st on right hand needle. Pick up and knit 2 sts at base of thumb. Knit across sts on left hand needle.

Next row: Purl, working P2tog over picked up sts at base of thumb. 36 {**40**} sts.

Cont even in Stripe Pat until work after ribbing measures 4³/4 {**5**1/4**}" [12 {**13**} cm], ending with a purl row.

Keeping cont of Stripe Pat, shape top as follows:

1st row: K1. Sl1. K1. psso. K12 {**14**}. K2tog. K2. Sl1. K1. psso. Knit to last 3 sts. K2tog. K1.

2nd row: Purl.

3rd row: K1. Sl1. K1. psso. K10 {**12**}. K2tog. K2. Sl1. K1. psso. Knit to last 3 sts. K2tog. K1.

4th row: Purl.

5th row: K1. Sl1. K1. psso. K8 (**10**). K2tog. K2. Sl1. K1. psso. Knit to last 3 sts. K2tog. K1.

6th row: Purl.

Cont in this manner, having 2 sts less between decs on next and every following alt row until there are 20 sts. Bind off purlwise.

Left Mitten: Work from ** to ** as given for Right Mitten.

Keeping cont of Stripe Pat, shape thumb gusset as follows:

1st row: K14 {**16**}. Inc 1 st in each of next 2 sts. Knit to end of row.

2nd row: Purl.

3rd row: K14 {**16**}. Inc 1 st in next st. K2. Inc 1 st in next st. Knit to end of row.

4th row: Purl.

5th row: K14 {**16**}. Inc 1 st in next st. K4. Inc 1 st in next st. Knit to end of row.

6th row: Purl.

Cont in this manner, having 2 sts more between incs for thumb gusset every alt row until there are 46 {**50**} sts.

Next row: Purl.

Make thumb: Next row: K26 {**28**}. **Turn.** Cast on 1 st. P12 (including cast on st). **Turn.** Cast on 1 st. Cont in Stripe Pat on these 13 sts for 2 {**2¼**}" [5 {**5.5**} cm], ending with a purl row.

Next row: K1. *K2tog. Rep from * to end of row. 7 sts. Break yarn leaving a long end. Draw end through rem sts and fasten securely. Sew thumb seam.

Work remainder of Mitten as given for Right Mitten.

Scarf

With larger needles and Dark Blue, cast on 33 sts.

1st row: (Right side). *K3. P3. Rep from * to last 3 sts. K3.

2nd row: *P3. K3. Rep from * to last 3 sts. P3.

3rd and 4th rows: As 1st and 2nd rows.

5th row: *P3. K3. Rep from * to last 3 sts. P3.

6th row: *K3. P3. Rep from * to last 3 sts. K3.

7th and 8th rows: As 5th and 6th rows.

These 8 rows form Check Pat.

Cont in Check Pat until work from beg measures approx 44" [112 cm], ending on a 4th or 8th row of Check Pat. Bind off in pat.

Fringe

Cut 12 inch [30.5 cm] lengths of Dark Blue, Blue, Red and Green. Taking 3 strands tog and crochet hook, knot into fringe across ends of Scarf in Stripe Pat (see Diagram). Trim fringe evenly.

Fringe Diagram

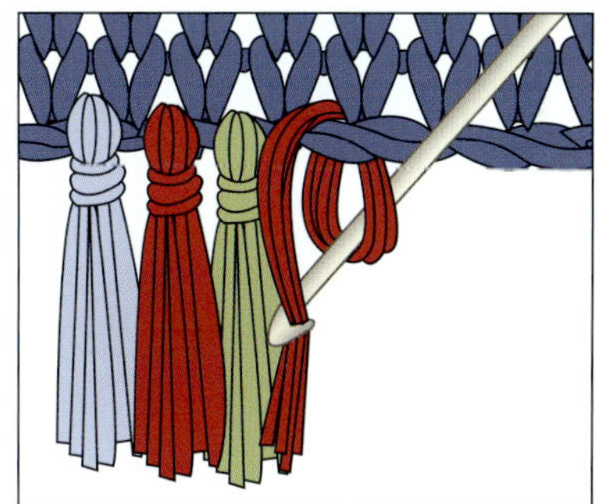

Single Crochet

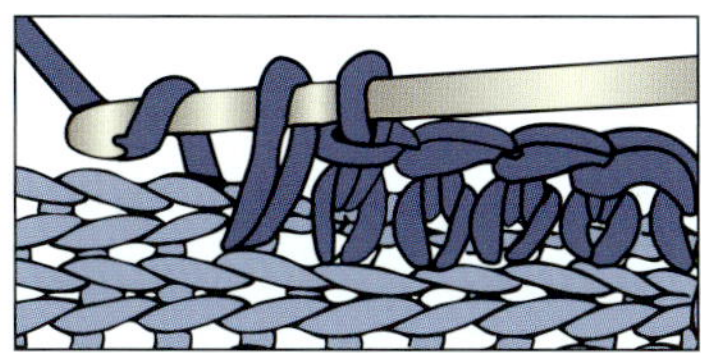

Reverse Single Crochet

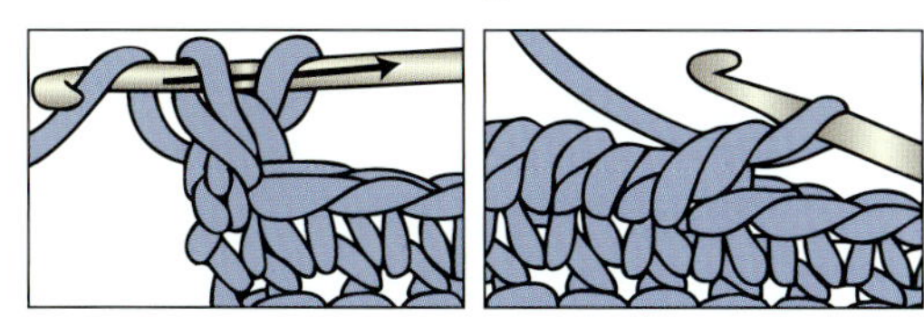

Twisted Cords

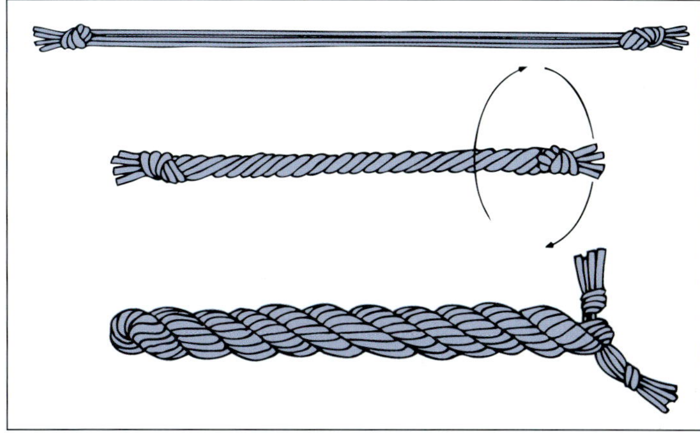

Funny Girl Set

EASY

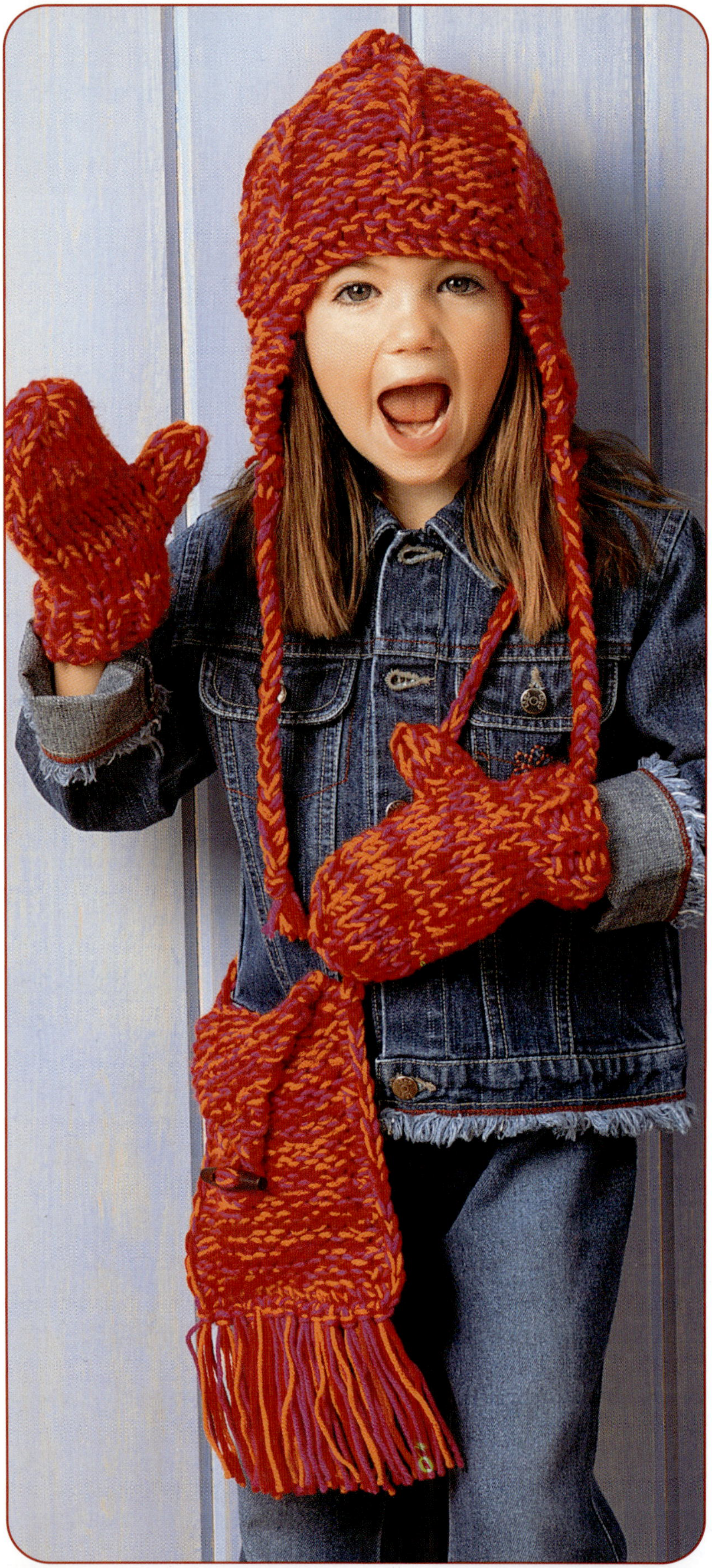

SIZES

Hat: One Size to fit child 4 to 8 years.

Mittens: To fit child 4 (**8**) years.

Bag: Approx 5" [12.5 cm] wide x 6" [15 cm] high.

MATERIALS

Sample made with
Patons® Canadiana (100 g / 3.5 oz)

4 MEDIUM

Main Color: #10728 Hot Fuchsia
Contrast A: #00072 Deep Orange
Contrast B: #00005 Cardinal

Size	4-8	years
HAT		
Main Color (MC) (Pink)	1	ball
Contrast A (Orange)	1	ball
Contrast B (Red)	1	ball
MITTENS		
Main Color (MC) (Pink)	1	ball
Contrast A (Orange)	1	ball
Contrast B (Red)	1	ball
SCARF		
Main Color (MC) (Pink)	1	ball
Contrast A (Orange)	1	ball
Contrast B (Red)	1	ball

Set of four size 8 mm (U.S. 11) knitting needles for Mittens and pair of size 8 mm (U.S. 11) and 10 mm (U.S. 15) knitting needles **or size needed to obtain gauge.** Size 6.5 mm (U.S. K or 10½) crochet hook and toggle for Bag.

GAUGE SWATCH

Hat: 9 sts and 14 rows = 4" [10 cm] in stocking st, with 3 strands of yarn and larger needles.

Mittens and Bag: 10 sts and 15 rows = 4" [10 cm] in stocking st, with 3 strands of yarn and smaller needles.

Funny Girl Set

alt = alternate
approx = approximately
cont = continue(ity)
dec = decrease
Inc = increase 1 stitch by knitting into front and back of next stitch
K = knit
K2tog = knit 2 stitches together
M1 = Make 1 st by picking up horizontal loop, lying before next st and knitting into back of it.

P = purl
P2tog = purl 2 stitches together
psso = pass slipped stitch over
rem = remaining
rep = repeat
rnd(s) = round(s)
Sl1 = slip next stitch knitwise
st(s) = stitch(es)
tog = together

INSTRUCTIONS

The instructions are written for the smaller size. If changes are necessary for larger size the instructions will be written thus { }. When only one number is given, it applies to both sizes. For ease in working, circle all numbers pertaining to your size.

Note: 3 strands of yarn (one from each ball of color) are used tog throughout.

Hat

Earflaps: (make 2)
With larger needles and 1 strand each of Pink, Orange and Red, cast on 3 sts.
Knit 2 rows.
Work in garter st (knit every row), inc 1 st each end of needle on next and following alt rows twice more. 9 sts.
Cont even in garter st until Earflap measures 3" [7.5 cm], ending with Wrong side facing for next row. Break yarn of First Earflap and leave all sts on a spare needle. **Do not** break yarn of Second Earflap.

Body of Hat: Joining row: With larger needles and 1 strand each of Pink, Orange and Red, cast on 4 sts. Knit these 4 sts. (K4. M1. K5) across Second Earflap. **Turn.** Cast on 16 sts. **Turn.** (K4. M1. K5) across First Earflap. **Turn.** Cast on 4 sts. 44 sts.
Work 4 rows in garter st.

Next row: (Right side). P4. (K1. P5) 6 times. K1. P3.
Next row: K3. (P1. K5) 6 times. P1. K4.
Rep last 2 rows until work from joining row measures 4" [10 cm], ending with Right side facing for next row.
Next row: P2. P2tog. (K1. P3. P2tog) 6 times. K1. P3. 37 sts.
Next row: K3. (P1. K4) 6 times. P1. K3.
Next row: P1. P2tog. (K1. P2. P2tog) 6 times. K1. P3. 30 sts.
Next row: K3. (P1. K3) 6 times. P1. K2.
Next row: P2. (K1. P1. P2tog) 7 times. 23 sts.
Next row: K2. (P1. K2) 7 times.
Next row: P2tog. (K1. P2tog) 6 times. K1. P2. 16 sts.
Next row: K2. (P1. K1) 7 times.
Next row: P1. (K2tog) 7 times. P1. 9 sts.
Next row: K1. P7. K1.
Next row: P1. (K2tog) 4 times. 5 sts.
Break yarn leaving a long end. Draw end through rem sts and fasten securely. Sew center back seam.

Ties: Cut 32 inch [81.5 cm] lengths of Pink, Red and Orange. Draw 3 lengths of each color through center of lower edge of Earflap. Divide strands into 3 groups, each group containing 2 strands of each color, and braid into Tie. Secure ends and trim evenly. (See Braid Diagram on page 13).

Mittens

Right Mitten: **With 1 strand each of Pink, Orange and Red, and set of four smaller needles, cast on 16 {**18**} sts. Divide sts on 3 needles. Join in rnd. Place marker on a first st.
1st rnd: (Right side). *K1. P1. Rep from * to end of rnd.
Last rnd forms (K1. P1) ribbing.
Work a further 4 {**5**} rnds in (K1. P1) ribbing.
Knit 4 {**6**} rnds.**

Shape thumb gusset: 1st rnd: K9 {**10**}. M1. K1. M1. Knit to end of rnd. 18 {**20**} sts.
2nd rnd: K9 {**10**}. M1. K3. M1. Knit to end of rnd. 20 {**22**} sts.
3rd rnd: K9 {**10**}. M1. K5. M1. Knit to end of rnd. 22 {**24**} sts.
4th rnd: K16. Slip last 7 sts just worked onto a safety pin (thumb opening). Knit to end of rnd.
5th rnd: Turn. Cast on 1 st over slipped sts. **Turn.** Knit to end of rnd. 16 {**18**} sts.

***Knit in rnds until work after ribbing measures 4¾ {**5¼**}" [12 {**13**} cm].
Rearrange sts as follows: 8 {**9**} sts on 1st needle. 4 sts on 2nd needle. 4 {**5**} sts on 3rd needle.

Shape Top: 1st rnd: *1st needle:* Sl1. K1. psso. Knit to last 2 sts. K2tog. ***2nd needle:*** Sl1. K1. psso. Knit to end of needle. **3rd needle:** Knit to last 2 sts. K2tog.
Dec 4 sts every rnd, as before, until there are 4 {**6**} sts. Break yarn. Thread ends through rem 4 {**6**} sts. Draw up and fasten securely.

Thumb: K7 from safety pin. Pick up and knit 1 st at base of thumb. Divide these 8 sts onto 3 needles.
Knit 4 rnds even.
Next rnd: (K2tog) 4 times. 4 sts.
Break yarn. Thread end through rem 4 sts. Draw up and fasten securely.***

Left Mitten: Work from ** to ** as given for Right Mitten.

Thumb gusset: 1st rnd: K6 {**7**}. M1. K1. M1. Knit to end of rnd.
2nd rnd: K6 {**7**}. M1. K3. M1. Knit to end of rnd.
3rd rnd: K6 {**7**}. M1. K5. M1. Knit to end of rnd.
4th rnd: K13 {**14**}. Slip last 7 sts just worked onto a safety pin (thumb opening).
5th rnd: K6 {**7**}. **Turn.** Cast on 1 st over slipped sts. **Turn.** Knit to end of rnd. 16 {**18**} sts.
Work from *** to *** as given for Right Mitten.

Bag
FRONT

****With smaller needles and 1 strand of each: Pink, Orange and Red, cast on 13 sts.
Beg with a purl row, work 21 rows in reverse stocking st.****
Bind off knitwise (Wrong side).

BACK

Work from **** to **** as given for Front.
Knit 5 rows (garter st).
Cont in garter st, dec 1 st each end of needle on next and every following alt row until there are 3 sts.
Work 3tog. Fasten off.

With 1 strand of each: Pink, Orange and Red and crochet hook, join 3 sides of Bag tog with 1 row of single crochet, working 3 single crochet in corners. **Do not fasten off.** Make a chain 31" [78.5 cm] long and join to first single crochet on opposite side. Fasten off.

Single Crochet

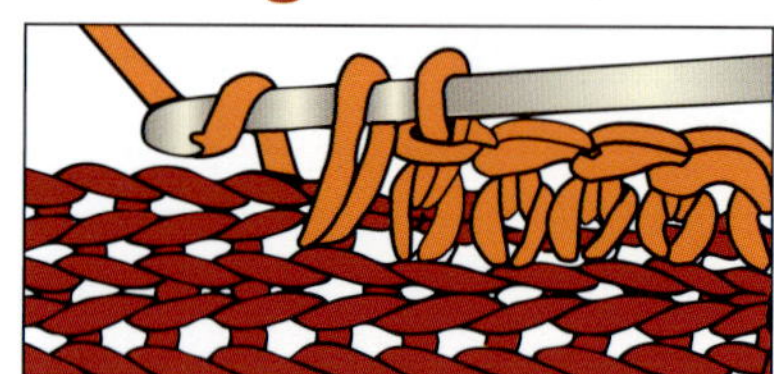

Button loop: With 1 strand of each: Pink, Orange and Red and crochet hook, join yarn with slip stitch at point of Bag. Chain 5. Join with slip stitch in same space as first slip stitch. Fasten off. Sew toggle to correspond to button loop.

Fringe: Cut 10" [25.5 cm] lengths of Pink, Orange and Red. Taking 3 strands tog, with crochet hook, knot into fringe across bottom of Bag (see Fringe Diagram). Trim fringe evenly.

Fringe Diagram

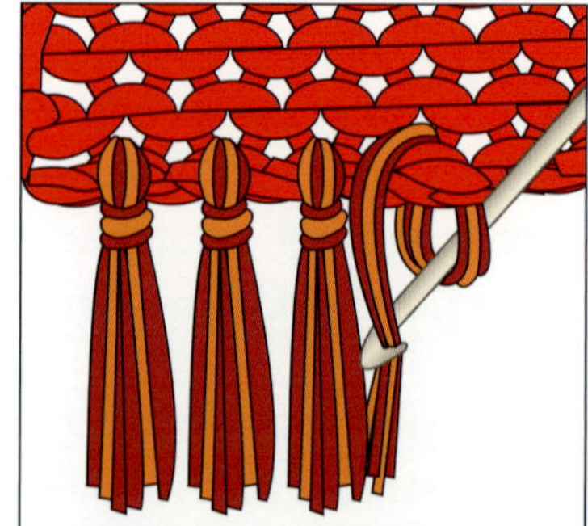

SIZES

Woman: One size to fit average lady.
Man: One size to fit average man.

MATERIALS

Sample made with Patons® Kroy Socks (50 g / 1.75 oz)

Main Color: #54008 Muslin
Contrast A: #54110 Norfolk Blue
Contrast B: #54040 Coal

Sizes	Woman	Man	
Argyle Version			
Main Color (MC) (Cream)	2	2	**balls**
Contrast A (Navy)	1	1	**ball**
Contrast B (Black)	1	1	**ball**
Plain Version *(not shown)*			
any color of your choice	2	2	**balls**

Size 3.25 mm (U.S. 3) knitting needles **or size needed to obtain gauge.**

GAUGE SWATCH

28 sts and 36 rows = 4" [10 cm] in stocking st.

ABBREVIATIONS

beg = beginning
cont = continue(ity)
inc = increase
K = knit
K2tog = knit 2 stitches together
M1 = make one st by picking up horizontal loop lying before next st and knitting into back of loop

P = purl
rem = remaining
rep = repeat
sts = stitch(es)

Argyle and Plain Gloves

The instructions are written for Woman's size. If changes are necessary for Man's size the instructions will be written thus { }. When only one number is given, it applies to both sizes. For ease in working, circle all numbers pertaining to your size.

Note: When working from chart, wind small balls of the colors to be used, one for each separate area of color in the design. Start new colors at appropriate points. To change colors, twist the two colors around each other where they meet, on Wrong side, to avoid a hole.

Argyle Version

RIGHT GLOVE: **With Cream, cast on 49 sts.
1st row: (Right side). K1. *P1. K1. Rep from * to end of row.
2nd row: P1. *K1. P1. Rep from * to end of row.
Rep these 2 rows of (K1. P1) ribbing for 3½" [9 cm] ending with Right side facing for next row. Work 2 {6} rows in stocking st.**

Make thumb gusset: 1st row: K1. Work 1st row of Chart I across next 25 sts, reading row from **right** to left. (K1. M1) twice. Knit to end of row.
Chart I is now in position.
Chart I is shown on page 24.
Work 3 rows even (working appropriate rows of Chart I), reading **knit** rows from **right** to left and **purl** rows from **left** to right.
Next row: K1. Work appropriate row of Chart I across next 25 sts. K1. M1. K3. M1. Knit to end of row.
Work 3 rows even (working appropriate rows of Chart I).

Cont in this manner, inc 1 st at each side of thumb gusset on next and every following 4th row until there are 61 sts.
Work 4 rows even (working appropriate rows of Chart I). 25 rows of Chart I are now complete. With Cream, purl 1 row.

Make thumb: 1st row: K40. **Turn.** Leave rem sts unworked.
2nd row: P13. **Turn.** Cast on 4 sts. 17 sts. Working on these 17 sts, work 20 {22} rows in stocking st.
Next row: K2tog. (K1. K2tog) 5 times.
Next row: Purl.
Next row: (K2tog) 5 times. K1.
Next row: Purl.
Break yarn. Thread end through rem sts. Draw up and fasten securely. Sew seam.

***With Cream and Right side of work facing, pick up and knit 5 sts from cast on sts at base of thumb. Knit to end of row. 53 sts.

Beg with a purl row, work 17 rows even in stocking st, ending with Right side facing for next row.***

Make 1st finger: Next row: K34. **Turn.**
Next row: P15. **Turn.** Cast on 2 sts. **Turn.** 17 sts. Work 24 {26} rows in stocking st.
Next row: (K2. K2tog) 4 times. K1.
Next row: Purl.
Next row: (K1. K2tog) 4 times. K1.
Next row: Purl.
Complete as given for thumb.

Make 2nd finger: With Right side of work facing and Cream, pick up and knit 3 sts at base of first finger. K7. **Turn.**
Next row: P17. **Turn.** Cast on 2 sts. **Turn.** 19 sts. Work 26 {28} rows in stocking st.
Next row: (K2. K2tog) 4 times. K3.
Next row: Purl.
Next row: (K1. K2tog) 5 times.
Next row: Purl.
Complete as given for thumb.

Make 3rd finger: With Right side of work facing and Cream, pick up and knit 3 sts at base of second finger. K7. **Turn.**
Next row: P17. **Turn.** Cast on 2 sts. **Turn.** 19 sts. Work 24 {26} rows in stocking st.

Next row: (K2. K2tog) 4 times. K3.
Next row: Purl.
Next row: (K1. K2tog) 5 times.
Next row: Purl.
Complete as given for thumb.

Make 4th finger: With Right side of work facing and Cream, pick up and knit 3 sts at base of third finger. K5. **Turn.**
Next row: P13.
Work 16 {**18**} rows in stocking st.
Next row: (K1. K2tog) 4 times. K1.
Next row: Purl.
Next row: (K2tog) 4 times. K1.
Next row: Purl.
Complete as given for thumb.
Sew side and cuff seam, reversing seam for cuff turnback.

LEFT GLOVE: Work from ** to ** as given for Right Glove.

Make thumb gusset: 1st row: K21. (M1. K1) twice. Work 1st row of Chart I to last st. K1.
Chart I is now in position.
Work 3 rows even (working appropriate rows of Chart I).
Next row: K21. M1. K3. M1. K1. Work appropriate row of Chart I to last st. K1.
Work 3 rows even (working appropriate rows of Chart I).

Cont in this manner, inc 1 st at each side of thumb gusset on next and every following 4th row until there are 61 sts.
Work 4 rows even (working appropriate rows of Chart I). 25 rows of Chart I are now complete.
With Cream, purl 1 row.

Make thumb: 1st row: K34. **Turn.** Cast on 4 sts. **Turn.**
2nd row: P17. **Turn.**
Complete as given for thumb of Right Glove.
Work from *** to *** as given for Right Glove.

Make 1st finger: Next row: K34. **Turn.** Cast on 2 sts. **Turn.**
Next row: P17. **Turn.**
Complete as given for 1st finger of Right Glove.

Make 2nd finger: With Right side of work facing and Cream, pick up and knit 3 sts at base of first finger. K7. Cast on 2 sts. **Turn.**
Next row: P19. **Turn.**
Complete as given for 2nd finger of Right Glove.

Make 3rd finger: With Right side of work facing and Cream, pick up and knit 3 sts at base of second finger. K7. Cast on 2 sts. **Turn.**
Next row: P19. **Turn.**
Complete as given for 3rd finger of Right Glove.

Make 4th finger: Work as given for 4th finger of Right Glove.
Sew side and cuff seam, reversing seam for cuff turnback.

Plain Version

Work as given for Argyle Version omitting all references to chart.

Chart I

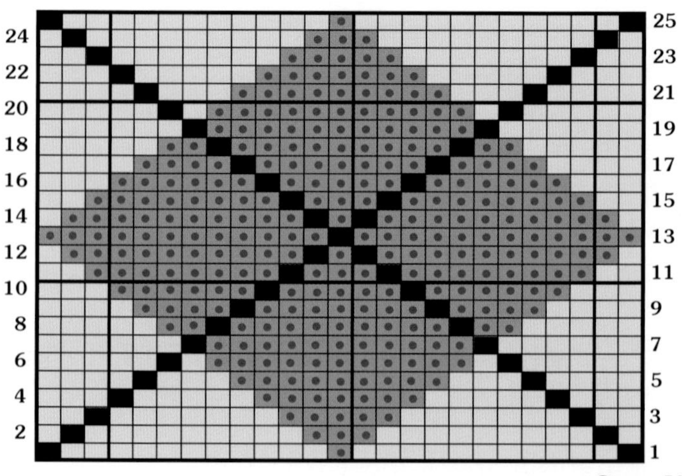

Key

SIZE

Finished Foot Length
One Adult Size to fit approx 10½" [26.5 cm].

MATERIALS

Sample made with Patons® Kroy Socks (50 g / 1.75 oz)

Main Color: #54008 Muslin
Contrast A: #54110 Norfolk Blue
Contrast B: #54040 Coal

Main Color (Cream)	2	balls
Contrast A (Navy)	1	ball
Contrast B (Black)	1	ball

Set of four double pointed knitting needles size 3.25 mm (U.S. 3) **or size needed to obtain gauge.**

GAUGE SWATCH

28 sts and 36 rows = 4" [10 cm] in stocking st.

ABBREVIATIONS

approx = approximately
cont = continue(ity)
inc = increase by knitting into front and back of next stitch
K = knit
K2tog = Knit 2 stitches together
P = purl
P2tog = purl 2 stitches together
psso = pass slipped st over
rem = remaining
rep = repeat
Sl1 = slip next stitch knitwise
st(s) = stitch(es)
tog = together

With Cream and 2 needles, cast on 74 sts **loosely.**

Work 4 " {10 cm} in (K1. P1) ribbing, inc 6 sts evenly across last row. 80 sts.

Note: When working from chart, wind small balls of the colors to be used, one for each separate area of color in the design. Start new colors at appropriate points. To change colors, twist the two colors around each other where they meet, on Wrong side, to avoid a hole.

Work Chart II in stocking st to row 12 of chart reading **knit** rows from **right** to left and **purl** rows from **left** to right.

Chart II is shown on page 12.

Next row: K1. K2tog. Work chart to last 3 sts. Sl1. K1. psso. K1.

Work 3 rows even from chart.

Rep last 4 rows to 60 sts.

Cont working Chart II to end of chart. Keeping cont of chart (beg at "2nd Start Here" position), work a further 25 rows. Break all yarns.

Arrange Heel Sts: Slip first 15 sts onto one needle. Slip last 14 sts onto another needle. Leave these 2 needles for heel. Put rem 31 sts onto another needle for instep.

With Wrong side of work facing, work center 31 sts of Chart II from row 26 of chart for a further 50 rows. Break yarns. Leave these sts on a spare needle.

Make heel: Slip all heel sts onto one needle. With Wrong side of work facing, join Cream to 29 heel sts and proceed as follows:

Next row: (Wrong side). K1. Purl to last st. K1.

Next row: *K1. Sl1. Rep from * to last st. K1.

Rep last 2 rows until heel measures 2½" [6 cm], ending with Right side facing for next row.

Shape heel: 1st row: K19. Sl1. K1. psso. **Turn.**

2nd row: P10. P2tog. **Turn.**

3rd row: K10. Sl1. K1. psso. **Turn.**

Rep last 2 rows until all sts have been worked. 11 sts rem. Break Cream.

Shape Instep and Make Sole: With Right side of work facing, Cream and first needle, pick up and knit 20 sts along left side of heel. With second needle, K11 of Heel. With third needle, pick up and knit 20 sts along right side of heel. 51 sts. Proceed as follows:

1st row: (Wrong side). K1. Purl to last st. K1.

2nd row: K1. K2tog. Knit to last 3 sts. Sl1. K1. psso. K1.

Rep last 2 rows until there are 27 sts.

Cont even until foot from picked up sts at heel measures same length as instep, ending with a Wrong side row.

Next rnd: K14 (this is 3rd needle). K13 (this is 1st needle). K31 from instep sts (this is 2nd needle). Join in rnd. Knit to end of 3rd needle. Slip 1 st from each end of 2nd needle onto 1st and 3rd needles. Sts are now divided as 14 sts on first needle, 29 sts on second needle and 15 sts on third needle.

Shape toe: 1st rnd: *1st needle:* Knit to last 3 sts. K2tog. K1. *2nd needle:* K1. Sl1. K1. psso. Knit to last 3 sts. K2tog. K1. *3rd needle:* K1. Sl1. K1. psso. Knit to end of needle.

2nd rnd: Knit.

Rep last 2 rnds until there are 26 sts divided as 6 sts on first needle, 13 sts on second needle and 7 sts on third needle. K6 from first needle onto third needle.

Graft 2 sets of 13 sts tog for toe (see Grafting Diagram on page 27).

Sew side seams of Instep and Sole. Sew back seam. Block on sock blockers or press lightly on Wrong side with a damp cloth.

Chart II

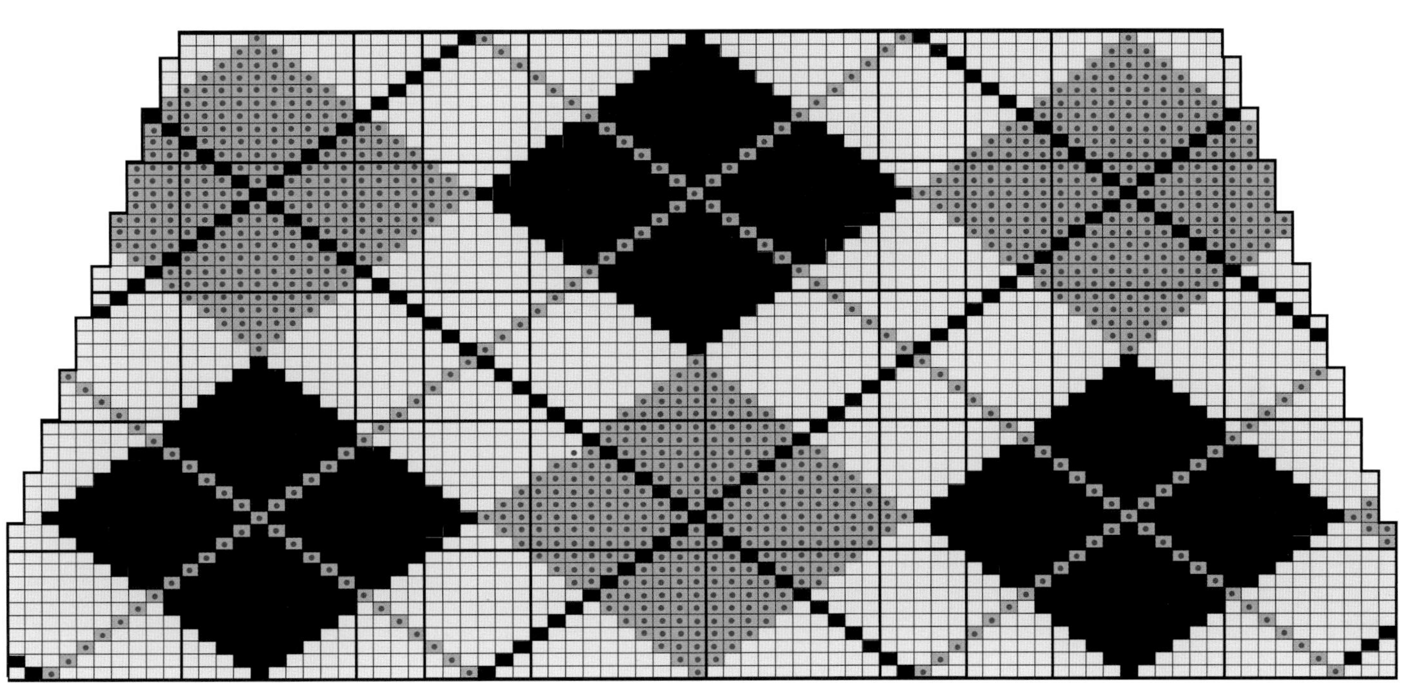

Key

Grafting

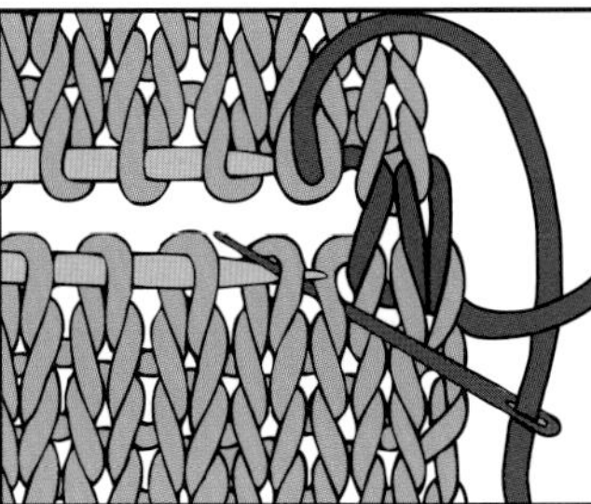
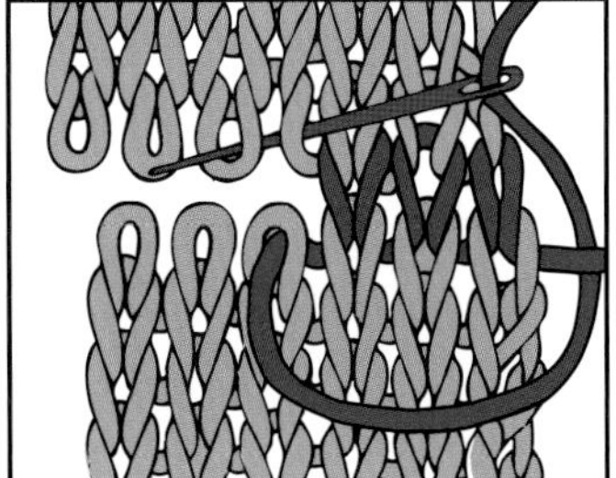

Fleur de Lis Bag

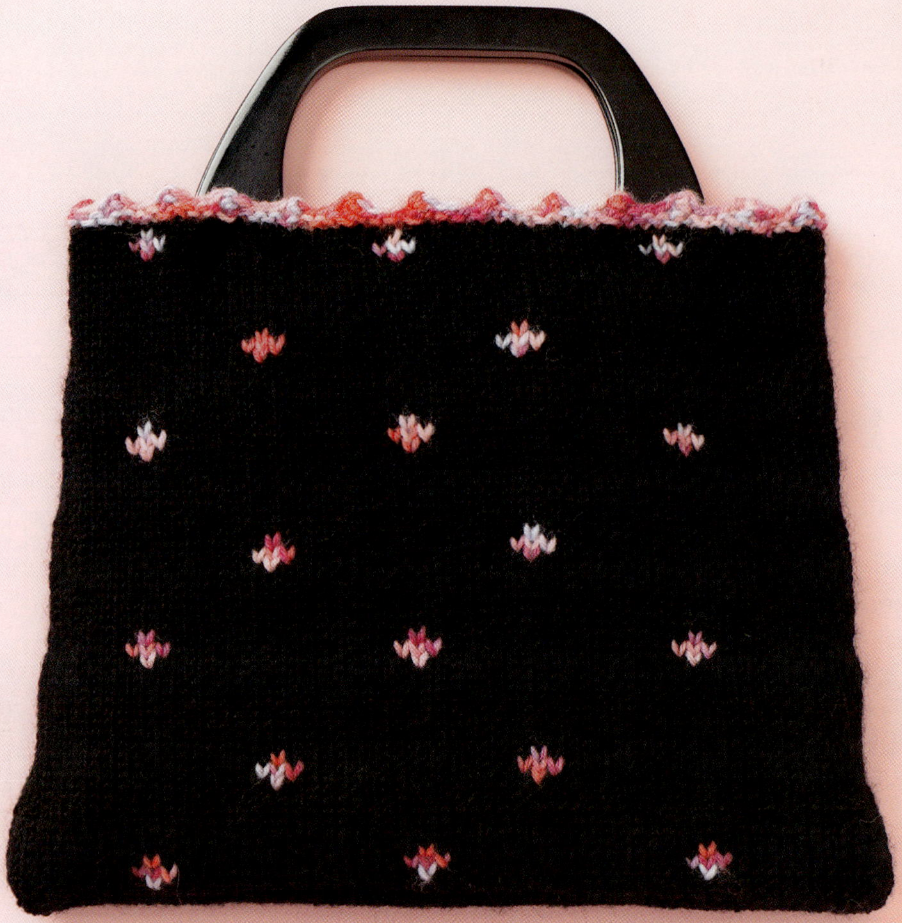

MEASUREMENTS

Approx 8¹/₂" x 7¹/₂" [21.5 x 19 cm].

MATERIALS

Sample made with Patons® Kroy Socks (50 g / 1.75 oz) 
Main Color: #54040 Coal
Contrast A: #54555 Fancy Free

Main Color (MC) (Black)	2	**balls**
Contrast A (Pink)	1	**ball**

Size 3.25 mm (U.S. 3) knitting needles **or size needed to obtain gauge**.
1 pair of 5" [13 cm] plastic handles. ³/₈ yard [0.4 m] of lining fabric.

GAUGE SWATCH

28 sts and 40 rows = 4" [10 cm] in stocking st.

Fleur de Lis Bag

approx = approximately
dec = decrease
K = knit
K2tog = Knit 2 stitches together
psso = pass slipped st over
rep = repeat
Sl1 = slip next stitch knitwise
st(s) = stitch(es)
tog = together

INSTRUCTIONS

BACK and **FRONT** (make alike).
With Black, cast on 65 sts.
Work 10 rows in stocking st.
Next row: K1. Sl1. K1. psso. Knit to last 3 sts. K2tog. K1.
Work 13 rows even in stocking st.
Rep last 14 rows 3 times more. 57 sts.

Next row: (Right side). With A, knit, dec 7 sts evenly across. 50 sts.
Next row: Knit.
Next row: (Picot row). Bind off 2 sts. *Cast on 2 sts. Bind off 6 sts. Rep from * to end of row.

With Pink, duplicate st Front as shown on Chart I.

FINISHING

Lining: Before sewing Front and Back tog, mark wrong side of lining according to Front and Back shapes with 3/4" [1.5 cm] seam allowance. Cut out lining pieces. Sew sides and bottom of lining pieces together using a French seam (see French Seam Diagram).
Sew Back and Front of Bag tog. Fold and stitch lining along top of Bag 1/2" [1 cm] from edge. Press lining to Wrong side along this stitching line. Attach handles to inside of Bag as shown in picture.

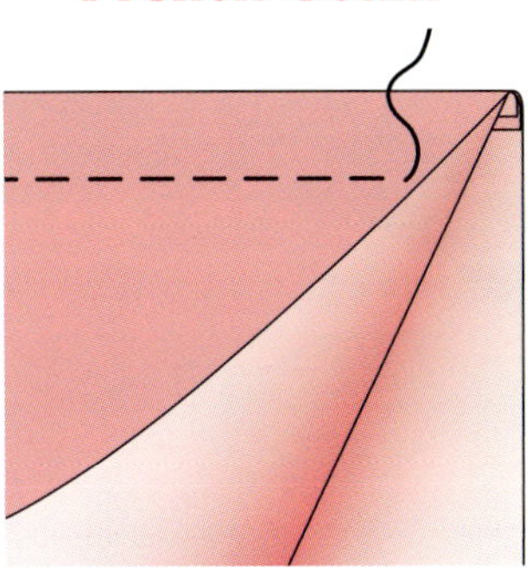

French Seam

With Wrong side tog stitch a seam 1/2 inch [1 cm] from edge. Trim this seam to 1/8 inch [3 mm] and press to one side. Fold fabric with Right side tog along seam line and press. Stitch a seam 1/4 inch [5 mm] from fold.

Duplicate Stitch

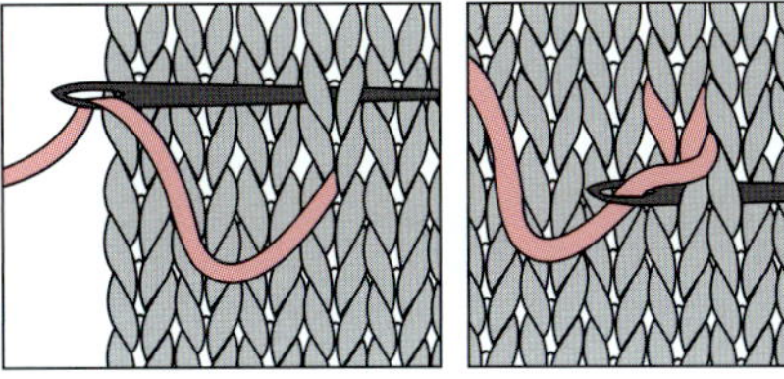

Chart I

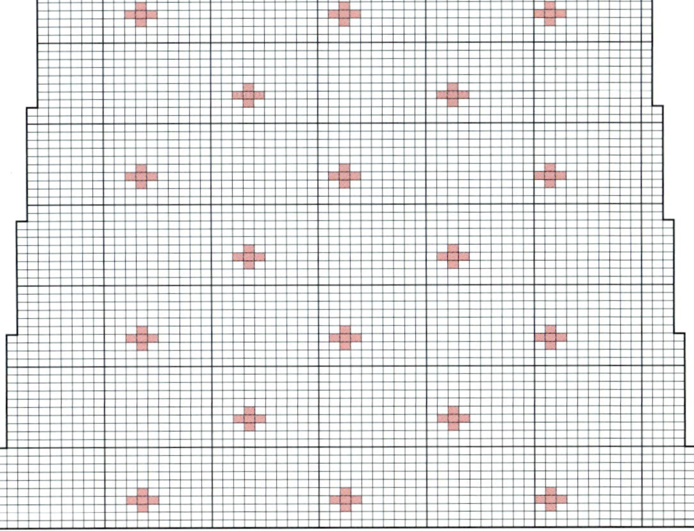

Key

☐ = Black

▨ = Pink

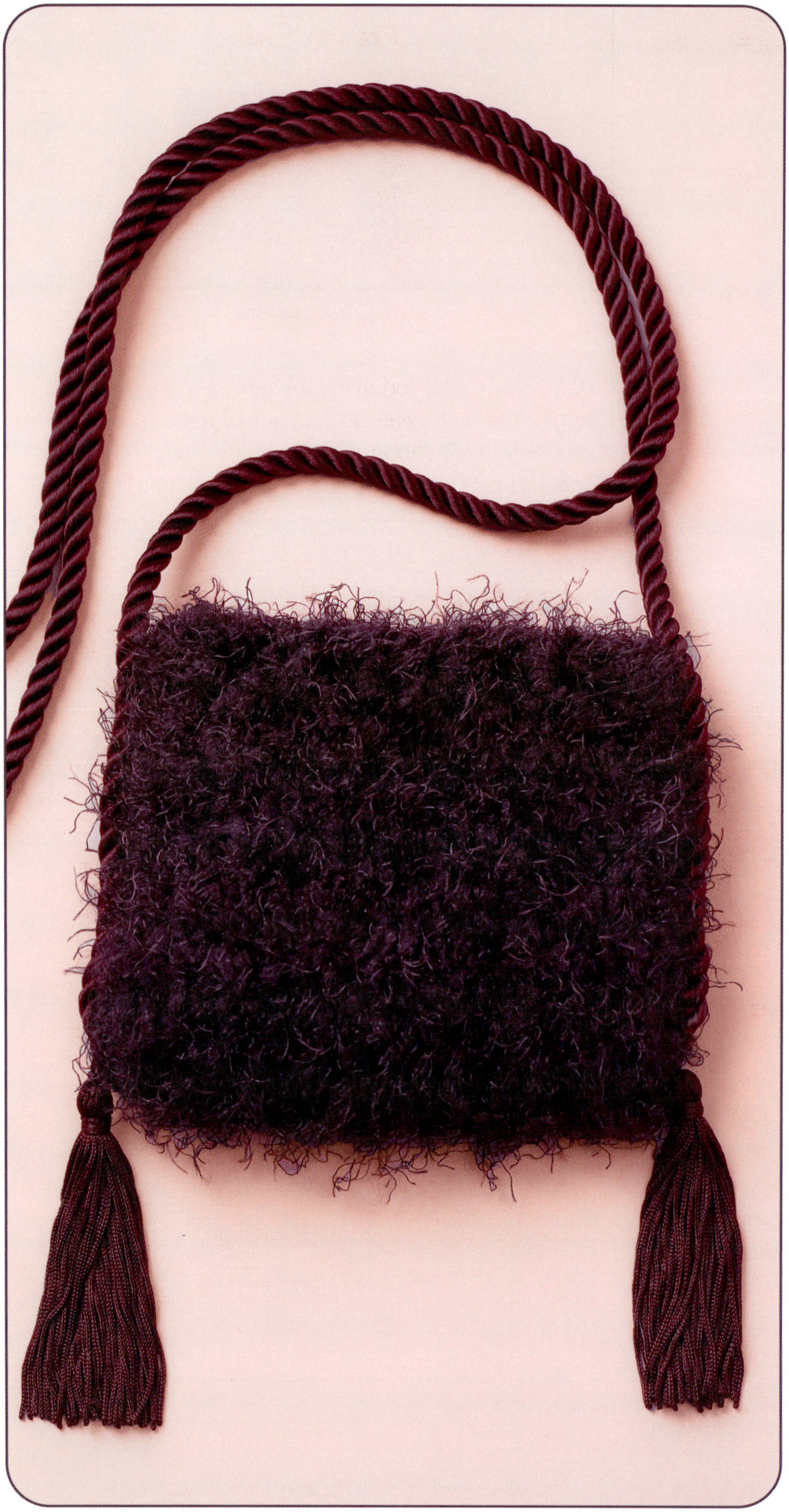

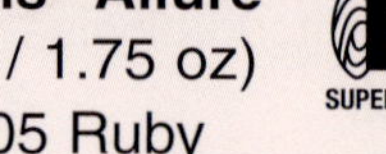

MEASUREMENTS

Approx 7" x 6" [18 cm x 15 cm].

MATERIALS

Sample made with Patons® Allure (50 g / 1.75 oz) #04405 Ruby 

Patons® Shetland Chunky (100 g / 3.5 oz) #03405 Deep Plum 

Patons® Allure (Dark Red)	**1 ball**
Patons® Shetland Chunky (Dark Purple)	**1 ball**

Size 11 mm (U.S. 17) knitting needles **or size needed to obtain gauge.** Drapery cord 1 yard [0.90 m] long. 2 tassels 2" [5 cm] long. 1/4 yard [0.2 m] of lining fabric. Snap fasteners.

GAUGE SWATCH

8 sts and 9 rows = 4" [10 cm] with 1 strand of each Patons® Allure and Patons® Shetland Chunky in stocking st.

ABBREVIATIONS

approx = approximately
beg = beginning
K = knit
P = Purl
pat = pattern
rep = repeat
st(s) = stitch(es)
tog = together

Enchanted Evening Bag

INSTRUCTIONS

FRONT and **BACK** (made in one piece)
Cast on 15 sts.
1st row: (Right side) K1. *P1. K1. Rep from * to end of row.
Rep last row twice more.
Next row: Knit.
Next row: Purl.
Rep last 2 rows until work from beg measures 11½" [29 cm], ending with Wrong side facing for next row.
Next row: K1. *P1. K1. Rep from * to end of row.
Rep last row twice more.
Bind off in pat.

FINISHING
Lining: Before sewing Front and Back tog, mark Wrong side of lining fabric according to Front and Back shape with ¾" [1.5 cm] seam allowance. Cut out lining piece. Sew sides of lining pieces together using a French seam (see French Seam Diagram).

With Right sides of Purse tog, fold work in half crosswise. Sew side seams leaving a ¼" [0.5 cm] opening at bottom for Cord. Tuck end of drapery cord into opening at bottom of side seam. Sew hole closed securely. Sew cord to side of Purse. Sew tassels to bottom corner of Purse as shown in picture.

Fold and stitch lining along top of Bag ½" [1 cm] from edge. Press lining to Wrong side along this stitching line. Sew snap fastener to inside of top edge.

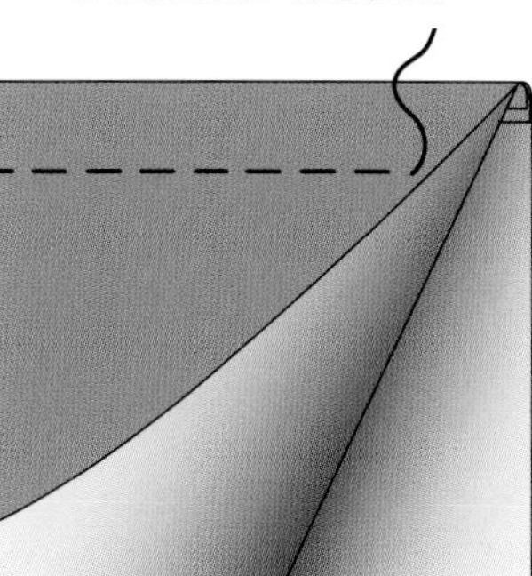

With Wrong side tog stitch a seam ½ inch [1 cm] from edge. Trim this seam to ⅛ inch [3 mm] and press to one side. Fold fabric with Right side tog along seam line and press. Stitch a seam ¼ inch [5 mm] from fold.

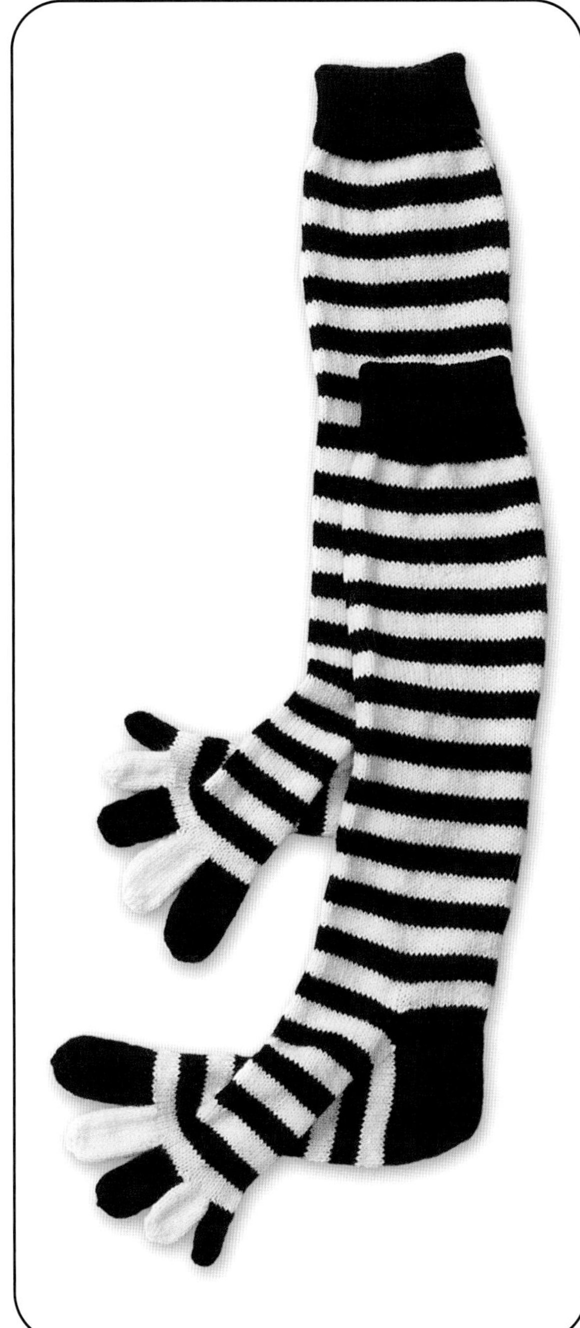

SIZES

Finished Foot Length

Child's Size 2-4	6"	[15	cm]
Child's Size 6-8	7½"	[19	cm]
Teen/Lady's	9½"	[24	cm]

MATERIALS

Sample made with Patons® Kroy Socks (50 g / 1.75 oz)

Main Color: #54040 Coal
Contrast A: #54006 Whitecap

Sizes	2-4	6-8	Teen/Lady's	
Main Color (Black)	2	2	3	balls
Contrast A (White)	1	1	2	ball(s)

Set of four double pointed knitting needles sizes 2.75 mm (U.S. 2) or two size 2.75 mm (U.S. 2) circular needles 16" [40 cm] long **or size needed to obtain gauge.**

GAUGE SWATCH

32 sts and 44 rows = 4" [10 cm] in stocking st.

ABBREVIATIONS

approx = approximately
cont = continue(ity)
K = knit
K2tog = Knit 2 stitches together
pat = pattern
P = purl
P2tog = purl 2 stitches

together
psso = pass slipped st over
rem = remaining
rep = repeat
rnd(s) = round(s)
Sl1 = slip next stitch knitwise
st(s) = stitch(es)

INSTRUCTIONS

The instructions are written for smallest size. If changes are necessary for larger sizes the instructions will be written thus { }. When only one number is given, it applies to both sizes. For ease in working, circle all numbers pertaining to your size

LEFT SOCK

With Black, cast on 54 {64**-76} sts loosely.** Divide sts into 18 {**20**-24} sts on first needle, 18 {**24**-28} sts on second needle and 18 {**20**-24} sts on third needle. Join in rnd, placing a marker on first st.

1st rnd: *K1. P1. Rep from * around.
Rep last rnd for 3½ {**4**-4½}" [9 {**10**-11.5} cm].

Proceed in Stripe Pat (knit 6 rnds in White and knit 6 rnds in Black) for 24 {**30**-30} rnds.

Shape leg: Keeping cont of Stripe Pat, proceed as follows:
Next rnd: *1st needle:* K1. Sl1K. K1. psso. Knit to end of needle. ***2nd needle:*** Knit. ***3rd needle:*** Knit to last 3 sts. K2tog. K1.
Work 18 {**18**-24} rnds even in Stripe Pat.

Keeping cont of Stripe Pat, rep last 19 {**19**-25} rnds 2 {**3**-3} times more. 48 {**56**-68} sts. 15 {**16**-20} sts on first needle, 18 {**24**-28} sts on second needle and 15 {**16**-20} sts on third needle.

Cont even in Stripe Pat until work after ribbing measures approx 9^{1}/$_{2}$ {**10^{1}/$_{2}$**-12^{1}/$_{2}$}" [24 {**26.5**-32} cm], ending with 6 rnds of White.

Arrange Heel sts: Slip last 3 {**2**-3} sts from end of first needle onto beg of 2nd needle. Slip first 3 {**2**-3} sts from beg of 3rd needle onto end of 2nd needle.
Rearrange 24 {**28**-34} sts from second needle onto 2 needles and leave for instep. Slip sts from third needle onto first needle for heel.

Make heel: With Wrong side of work facing, join Black to 24 {**28**-34} heel sts and proceed as follows:
Next row: (Wrong side). K1. Purl to last st. K1.
Next row: *K1. Sl1. Rep from * to last 2 sts. K2.
Rep last 2 rows until heel measures 1^{3}/$_{4}$ {**2**-2^{1}/$_{2}$}" [4.5 {**5**-6} cm], ending with Wrong side facing for next row.

Shape heel: 1st row: P12 {**14**-17}. P2tog. P1. **Turn.**
2nd row: K3. Sl1. K1. psso. K1. **Turn.**
3rd row: P4. P2tog. P1. **Turn.**
4th roe: K5. Sl1. K1. psso. K1. **Turn.**
5th row: P6. P2tog. P1. **Turn.**
6th row: K7. Sl1. K1. psso. K1. **Turn.**

7th row: P8. P2tog. P1. **Turn.**
8th row: K9. Sl1. K1. psso. K1. **Turn.**
9th row: P10. P2tog. P1. **Turn.**
10th row: K11. Sl1. K1. psso. K1. **Turn.**

Size 2-4 only: 11th row: P14.

Sizes 6-8 and Teen/Lady's only: 11th row: P12. P2tog. P1. **Turn.**
12th row: K13. Sl1. K1. psso. K1. **Turn.**

Size 6-8 only: 13th row: P16.

Size Teen/Lady's only: 13th row: P14. P2tog. P1. **Turn.**
14th row: K15. Sl1. K1. psso. K1. **Turn.**
15th row: P16. P2tog. P1.
16th row: K17. Sl1. K1. psso.

All Sizes: Shape Instep: With Right side of work facing, Black, and first needle, pick up and knit 12 {**14**-18} sts along left side of heel. With second needle, knit across 24 {**28**-34} sts for instep. With third needle, pick up and knit 12 {**14**-18} sts along right side of heel. Knit first 7 {**8**-9} sts from heel onto end of third needle. Slip rem 7 {**8**-9} sts from heel onto beg of first needle. 62 {**72**-88} sts are now divided as 19 {**22**-27} sts on first needle, 24 {**28**-34} sts on second needle and 19 {**22**-27} sts on third needle.
1st rnd: *1st needle:* Knit to last 4 sts. K2tog. K2. ***2nd needle:*** Knit. ***3rd needle:*** K2. Sl1K. K1. psso. Knit to end of needle.
2nd rnd: Knit.
Keeping cont of Stripe Pat, rep last 2 rnds until there are 48 {**52**-60} sts divided as 12 {**12**-13} sts on first needle, 24 {**28**-34} sts on second needle and 12 {**12**-13} sts on third needle.

Cont even until foot from picked up sts at heel measures approx 4 {**5**-6^{1}/$_{4}$}" [10 {**12.5**-16} cm], ending with 6 rnds of White.